Happy Christmas 2021 Mum.

Much love

Valerie, Peter
+ Harvey
x

Poetry in Minutes

By Malcolm Judd

ISBN: 978-109-166-9284
© Copyright © 2019 Malcolm Judd

All rights reserved. No part of this publication may be reproduced,
distributed, or transmitted in any form or by any means,
including photocopying, recording, or other electronic or mechanical methods,
without the prior written permission of the publisher,
except in the case of brief quotations embodied in critical reviews and
certain other non-commercial uses permitted by copyright law.
For permission requests, contact the publisher at the address below.

FORWORD

"Mac has been a friend for many many years and that makes me very lucky. Mac has a very special talent with his words, that he turns into amazing poetry. His poetry brings joy to many people, whether it is in memory of someone, or the changing seasons and nature. I feel honoured that I have been asked to write this dedication to him." Lynn Daborn.

ACKNOWLEDGEMENTS

I would like to thank everyone who has supported me in this quest to get my work published; I could not have done it without your help. All poems except for guest submissions are written by the author.

Guest poems submitted by;

The Innocent Knife: Katie Ricketts
A Child's Bedtime Story: My Son

Poetry in Minutes

THE RIVER

The wisps of the weeping willow
Caress the surface of the old river
Like a paint brush stroke in mid flow
Cutting a pattern sharp as a glass sliver

Mallards paddle their webbed feet at speed
But advance so slowly in the mainstream
A cormorant dives to the depths to feed
Paddle boat cruisers at full steam

The meandering waterway takes its course
Through valleys and hills so green
The mighty wiers spew water with force
While countryside beauty remains serene

A royal swan glides as though on air
Geese gaggle loudly at one another
Down on the riverbank I haven't got a care
I love to be here more than any other

COUNTRY MAMA

Colours so vibrant such a wonderful sight
Odours of dirt soaked rain a warm damp night
Undulating landscapes smothered in green
Nothing like this countryside have we seen

Trees that dance in a light warm breeze
Rivers full of life swans that glide with ease
Yet there is silence in this countryside of life
Marvellous peace away from trouble and strife

Allow yourself to drink in the awesome delight
Making the most of each magical day and night
Always share the beauty that you discover
County Mama your quite like no other

AWAKENING

As I sit here in the early morning light
Awaiting the rising of the sun
The dawn chorus is being sung with delight
Another new day in my life has begun

Cotton wool clouds propelled by a soft breeze
Distant sounds of wilderness waking
I could stay in this moment with relative ease
My favourite time of day is as dawn is breaking

Crimson red skies fill with the traces of craft
On a journey to some exotic location
Their metallic shells alight as they cross the sun's path
Scarring the atmosphere as they speed to their destination

Suddenly everything comes to life once more
As though it has slept for many years
The beauty and grace of birds as they soar
On the horizon at last the full golden sun appears

My face is warmed gently by the streaming rays
Awakening my soul as I wonder at the sight
I welcome the new morning on every single day
Until it burns itself out then I welcome the night

A YEARS JOURNEY

With spring the beauty returns once more
Each passing day life awakens from the cold
Thoughts of warmer days come to the fore
The longer evening light begins to unfold

The vibrant colours of heather appear
Flooding vast bare mountainous lands
Before we realise it summer is here
Picnic season on beaches golden sands

Autumn arrives too soon you might say
With its own beauty and delights
Short sharp showers are the order of the day
Sultry evenings turn into dark cold nights

The unforgiving winter arrives in earnest
Only the sturdy thistle can withstand
A year has passed what an amazing journey
I dream of the day when I return to Scotland

THE LIVING WATER

The early morning mist
rolls ghostly across the lake
Cobwebs shimmer above the dewy grass
so silent yet alive

In the depths a lonely grey figure
Awaits its prey
The small yet sprightly fish
Darts closer to its life's end

With a thrash if his powerful tail
The majestic pike strikes

The lake lives

The waters fall silent once more
As tiny ripples dance towards the shore
A leaf upon the glass like water
Skims gently propelled by a warm breeze

A kingfisher sits statue like
Searching for fry in the shallows

All too soon the golden sun
lowers in the darkening sky
And although the day may be coming to an end
The lake lives on into the night
Protecting its life beneath the surface

REMEMBERING A BABY DAUGHTER

Your baby is still with you alive in your heart
Because of this you will never be apart
The precious daughter which you have lost
Will always be remembered whatever the cost

Think of her often not with sadness or regret
But with love adoration for you will never forget
She was and is your beautiful baby girl
Imagine her now hair all wispy and curls

The cuddles you gave her to last a lifetime
Implanted in her heart though it seems sublime
Your Daughter looks down she cruises the stars
All she wants is for you to heal those scars

Remember fondly your daughter with love
Be peaceful knowing she watches from above
 She still has a place as she did from the start
Your baby daughter is alive in your heart

RAP

I close my eyes but sleep doesn't come to me all i can think of is what life has done to me i been depressed been so down i've forgotten how to smile i only know how to frown i feel like i'm gonna drown but through it all you been there for me showing me someone cares for me Now here i am at the end of it all a better person having taken a fall this is my time this is my call to tell others it ain't all BAD Now i close my eyes and i fall asleep your arms around me yours forever to keep my life is better than it was before cos i have you makin me feel secure that i'm not alone anymore Because of you my life has changed because of you i'm no longer in chains this is my story i need to tell i am a person who's come back from hell Because of you i smile again because of you it never rains my life is complete i don't need no more cos of you i feel secure that i aint alone anymore This is my time this is my call to try to tell others it ain't all BAD This is my story i need to tell i am a person who's come back from hell this is my time this is my call to tell others it ain't all BAD!

HAPPY MOTHER'S DAY

Happy mother's day I wish to you
You loved and cared for me as I grew
All these years have passed since you have gone
Though missed each day life has gone on

I still chat to you when things get tough
I still tell you when I am feeling rough
You are still with me in my heart
That way we will never be apart

So Happy Mother's day even if your not here
I am thinking of you wiping away a tear
I hope you are proud of who I have become
All I want to say is I love you mum

Happy Mother's day mum I love you, I miss you
Lots of love always your son

I THANK YOU ALL

This year has been pretty damn tough
Mental health issues and feeling rough
But I have had so much good support
From friends I have known for years
For me they have all strongly fought

You know who you are
Too many for me to mention
But take it from me from my heart
You all have eased my stress and tension

So here I am I have come through
And mainly it is with thanks to you
The people who matter and care about me
Are the ones who have helped
To set me free

From my heart I thank you all
For coming to my side
When depression called
So take my thanks with all my love
To all of you who have helped me recover
It means the world to me
You shine as bright as the stars above
My appreciation for you all
Is above any other

TRUTH

There are so many different conflicting views
Lies and stories making us believe untruths
Take time just to think for yourself
To realise the fight is not worth the fight itself

If we can believe in only what we know
And act upon fact not fiction only then can we grow
To appreciate each other for what we are worth
To grasp our short lived life whilst upon this earth

Listen to your heart and follow it through
And be amazed by what you will find to be true
Realise your potential in every single last minute
And you will find a peace your love within it

Forget what is taught by wrongdoing and hate
Live your life happy within a peaceful state
For what we do now reflects on us all
Take up the challenge rally to the call

LOVE is THE most important thing
Let it take you over making your heart sing
Remember that only you have the power
Let this one short life be your finest hour

DO NOT BE DEFINED

Do not be defined by an illness
Whatever that may seem to be
It does not make you a person of less
Remarkability search your heart you'll see

For you are who you are within your soul
So grip on to the strength within you there
Take a positive step reach for a reachable goal
Then you will see yourself free without a care

Believe in yourself and you will reach the light
This long dark tunnel does not go on forever
Trust yourself know what you believe to be right
A helping hand I offer you we'll get there together

So remember this you are who you are
No one can put you down and out
For we are the ones who look to the future far
We are the ones without a doubt

Take strength in the knowledge you are unique
But that does not mean you are alone
I like you am my worst critic
I like you walk into the unknown

I will recover as I assure you you will too
Then look out world we will conquer and discover
I believe this to be the truth I am but one of few
But we are not on our own for we have each other

TOGETHER AS ONE

All of you all here together as one
Respect and honour counts for so much
When all the talking is over and done
You are the ones to never lose touch

Old school values these days seem lost
New generations do not understand
Whatever it takes whatever the cost
Brothers together hand in hand

A common bond back in the day
To make a stand together just and right
This I still will always do I have to say
In the shadow of the sun and the dark of the night

Now there are some who will always be
Though they are but just a few
I feel Included and welcomed you clearly see
My respect and honour I happily give to you

RAIN

Mirror reflections of rain soaked stone
Moody skies broken by beams of light
Dark colours in a hue of two tone
Captured in a moment of perceived sight

Shadowy trees stand tall in the sky
Towering above the damp soft ground
Droplets of water from clouds which cry
Mother nature never fails to astound

BE STRONG

Be strong in your defiance
For this time will end
There will be time for songs and dance
So stay with it my brave friend

There will be times you feel low
With no money in your bank
But remember just go with the flow
For you have plenty for which you can thank

Friends are there sometimes not
But you are never alone
For the ones who love you a lot
Are the ones who stay after you've grown

Keep up that chin never look down
You do so much for everyone
Keep that smile and never frown
You will do all that needs to be done

So take it from me I know this well
This life can be so terribly hard
But you will succeed I can tell
Because you my friend are an ace card

HAPPY BIRTHDAY

Enjoy your day of celebration and fun
Happy birthday wishes from everyone
Another year older but still so young
Happy Birthday to you a song is sung

Your beautiful family and you
Should have fun the whole day through
To be a mum such a special time of life
Make the most if now without trouble or strife

So this evening on your extra special day
Enjoy it so much in each and every way
Happy Birthday have a great day
I wish you happiness in each and every way

CAR MEET

Shutter Gang time for a car meet
Loaded Engines ripping the street
Showing your passion under the hood
It's happening down here it's gonna be good

Trace your hands across my paint
Feel the rhythm style sorry it ain't
Dressed up bodies wheels so proud
We are Shutter Gang revving up loud

So come on with your Vauxhall or Sport
Everyone welcome no matter what sort
Have a banging time down on the street
When you come to a Shutter Gang meet

THE COAST

White topped waves crash upon jagged rock
Cliffs battered by charging seas of power
Walls of stone protecting ships at dock
The tides relentless stronger by the hour

Windswept sand upon the paths and grass
Seagulls screaming chasing one another
Chanting their song as they glide past
A child clings tightly to its mother

Flagpole ropes clatter in an increasing breeze
Promenade beams of subdued light
How I love the roughness of the seas
Drinking in its beauty from dawn till night

For all its wildness and destruction of coast
My heart yearns for an endless stream
Of beachcombing days I adore the most
To live by the sea is my perfect dream

DEPRESSION

I do not want your sympathy
Nor do I need you to understand
All I ask is that you show a little empathy
When depression takes my hand

Do not cross the road to avoid my path
Or whisper so that I may not hear
I only want a chat and a laugh
My friendship to still be held dear

The illness which lies deep within my mind
Cannot be seen by you or anyone
But take the time to talk, do not be blind
Do not be scared of me please do not run

I do not want to lose my family my friends
Just because of my mental health
The deep dark hole into which I descend
Cannot be filled with luxury or wealth

So next time you see me please say hi
It may not be as scary as you may think
I will be honest with you and never lie
A friend is all I need so that I do not sink

VOICES

The voices that speak within your head
Are not who you really are
Maybe they are from the past
A mask to cover your scars

They talk to you and tell you things
Which really are not true
You have the strength the inner power
To overcome them and to re become you

So never give up believing your true worth
Nor the fact the reason that you are on this earth
To bring happiness and joy to all you meet
You are the kind I believe who is not to be beat.

THE INNOCENT KNIFE
By Katie Ricketts

I hear the screams of the pain they bring
I feel the warm blood on my blade
And Yet
I am helpless

I cannot run and hide from my mistakes
I cannot take refuge
Yet I am forced
To own up to what I have done

But yet I am the innocent one
For I am the knife who has no chance in life
No hopes
No dreams

I do not wish to be a killer a death machine
I am apologetic to whom I have injured internally
But I am not the guilty one in this crime

For I am the Innocent Knife

I WISH

I wish I could sing a beautiful song
Of life all good and never any wrong
I wish I could make everyone smile
Remove their sadness for a short while

I wish I could play an instrument of sound
To bring people together from all around
I wish I could do more than I ever thought
Just to show the love I have brought

I wish I could bring calm and peace to all
Make troubles vanish but most of all
I wish you love and luck in all you do
I wish happiness your whole life through

JANUARY

The beginning of the year is full of delight
Frosty chilly days the long freezing cold night
Snow tipped mountains leafless trees
Beauty can be found in all of these

The Small Crested Tit always grateful to feed
On garden bird tables replenished with seed
Feather crowned heads a royal bird in flight
These pretty birds are such a rare sight

New year's resolutions that never seem to last
Memories of Christmas which went too fast
A new adventure which now has begun
Happy New Year's wishes to everyone

WE FOUGHT FOR YOU

We fought for our Country and our Queen
You would never believe
Some of the things that we have seen
From young children carrying a gun

To an old woman crying over a loved one
We fought to protect you and still do
All we ask is compassion and understanding
To help us recover when we come home to you

Instead of leaving us like thrown away trash
Like you don't care so arrogant so brash
We fought for you so help us when home
We do not want to feel unloved nor alone

This is not too much we are asking of you
All we need is some time some respect
This will help us recover and get through
We fought for you now is your time

To give us the help we need let us draw the line
No more shall we be ignored and left
All we have been through
The life the death

We fought for you now fight for us
No more shall we be covered up nor crushed
This is all we ask this holds true
To fight for us like we fought for you

A CHILD'S DREAM
A short story written by my Son

The end of another day but the beginning of a little boy's bedtime routine, all tucked up in bed thinking about all that has happened, and all that has been said.

Dad picks up their favourite book with the cardboard all creased down the spine, showing how loved it is.

Dad sits on the edge of the bed as the boy settles down and drifts off to dreamland while listening to his dad's voice, while comforted by the familiar tones.

The last words in the boys mind quietly repeats...

Snowy hat snowy....

Suddenly the boy is surrounded by snow, not cold and raw but the fluffy type, powdery. You know, like the dusted white powder all over mum's sponge cakes.

The little one spins around on the spot taking in the sights of the beautiful white landscape and the mountains.

Then... stops...

His eyes landing on a deer and its young in the distance. "Wait for me" the little one calls..."Wait for me!!"

Getting closer and closer to the mountains the deer fade into the distance, like a mirage but in reverse, and in snow rather than in the unforgiving heat of a desert, but the child is still there, completely calm, no fear.

A familiar and much loved voice drifts in on the cool wind until the child hears it all around him as if it is being broadcast from all the twinkling stars in the sky, like they are billions of tiny twinkling speakers.

Rise and shine... then louder... rise and shine...

The voice gets louder and as it does the mountains and snow begin to fade away into the darkness.

The child knows this doesn't belong, this part is not part of the snowy mountain song.

This part is different, "How could it be getting dark when all he can hear is... "Rise and Shine"

And, as if by magic, the snow was gone and the child was back in his bed with daddy saying... "Rise and shine little one it is a brand new day, rise and shine."

PAUL
In loving memory

Paul Michael Allan Daborn
09/02/1990 - 02/03/1990

From the moment you took your first breath
To the second you took your last
Your innocent love lies within us forever
Even though your physical remains in the past

There is not a day which passes us by
That we wish that you were here
And although the hands of time go on
In our hearts we will forever love you dear

Sleep well now our darling sweet pea
You will never be forgotten by anyone
We know that you are happy and blessed
Being a part of heavens home our darling son

So don't be afraid and never forget
Mummy and Daddy love you so much
Only the time without you here
Is our one and only regret

Bless you sweet Paul our darling baby boy
We know you are cared for in heaven above
Even though you are gone never to return
We keep your memory alive with all of our love

GOOD MORNING

Blue cloudless skies an ocean of light
Rose petal pink hue a sunrise so bright
A breeze soft like a feather on skin
Good morning world let this day begin

Diamond droplets on dew tipped grass
I have awoken from a dreamland passed
Birds call their bright good morning song
For moments like these I yearn I long

Lost within this glorious beauty of dawn
Mesmerized by the magical early morn
I relish this very moment this very minute
The gift of our beautiful world and all within it

SPRING

Spring is coming
Thank goodness for that
No more warm jumpers
No more woolly hat

T shirts and shorts
Will be the things that are in
In the warm sunshine
No more the early dark evening

Oh how i've missed the hazy sunny days
Bright blue skies warm sultry nights
Colourful flower beds breathing new life
The joys of springs amazing sights

Time to celebrate I cannot wait
For this is my favourite time of year
Everything alive in vibrant beauty
Goodbye to winter spring is nearly here

MY THOUGHTS

Today is a new day for yesterday has passed
Not forgotten with all that took place
Memories imprinted like a shadow that is cast
We shall continue with honour love and grace

In the morning the sun will rise once more
The tides will arrive and again they will depart
We will journey onward our pride to the fore
Find and share the love lying within your heart

Let us not be broken by sadness anger or hate
But instead use our strength for each other
To end the sadness as it is never too late
Whether you're a son daughter father or mother

Teach the future of society that we all belong
Regardless of gender religion or colour
To hate divide or kill that is surely so wrong
But love understand and respect all others

MY thoughts are for me but I wanted to share
As I believe we WILL rise free from this rage
I need to let everyone know that I CARE
so for you I pour my HEART out on this page

RIVERS

Babbling rivers winding through vales
Waterfalls tumbling up in the dales
Transforming the landscape near and far
Providing a home for dace chub and char

Beautiful scenery of trees and fields of green
Hills of sheep grazing a country scene
Through towns and cities country wide
Rivers streaming gold dust as they glide

Warm waters of the lower lands
Ice streams that freeze your hands
Pretty locks giving way to boats
Ferrying all manners if things including goats

Remember in the countryside to respect
Nature's beauty never to neglect
For if we don't it will not last
We will return to nothing like the past

DO THE RIGHT THING

Do the right thing is the aim
To help others, it's not a game
All the good that is done
All the bad is overcome

Giving good advice and great ideas
Is music to everyone's ears
Heartfelt gifts from a millionaire
Showing the world how he cares

Happiness is all I really feel
It makes me realise life is real
So keep up with the good you do
Being honest straight and true

Thank you Do The Right Thing
You really do make my heart sing
My respect for you is truly real
This is how I really feel

FEBRUARY

Glass like water shrouded by mountain mist
The late rising sun a sight of pure bliss
Star crossed lovers gaze to the skies
With love and adoration within their eyes

A frisky Mountain Hare bounds over the plain
Scurrying in the heather through hail and rain
His elongated ears and large flat feet
Make this majestic mammal one of the elite

28 days short 29 a leap year every four
Spring almost upon us so begins the thaw
Though a short month in the calendar year
February is one in which we hold our hearts dear

PETANQUE

The sport of petanque is a funny old game
With lots of strange rules and stranger names
Lead second skip pointer shooter but a few
Tactics and pure skill an eye that throws true

Hopefully, most of the time well,
ok now and then, oh what the hell
We play we always have fun
As a team we always play as one

Clashing of metal the shingle flies
The league cup and friendly ties
Sunny summer evenings we often hope
Mostly rain and wind but we still cope

Tactics and skill are both sort after
A serious measure a joke some laughter
Make no mistake we take pride in our game
But we have lots of fun all the same

NO TIME

Though the time has been but short
It's time for you to move on
You seem to me to be a loving kind sort
And I shall miss you when you are gone

Follow your dreams whether your heart or head
Do not allow others to shadow your mind
Do not be what others want but yourself instead
Honest, caring but most of all kind

Look to the future with an open mind
Never look back and regret
For that way happiness you will surely find
And the best is definitely to come yet

So my face may be sad that you have to part
To find your meaning within this life
I wish you nothing but a happy heart
And a future without trouble or strife

9/11

9/11 a day I will never forget
The lost the loved the heroes all
In my memory forever this date is set
Strong together this world shall not fall

No matter how much they try
With their bombs guns bullets and knives
We may weep and uncontrollably cry
They shall never win ruin our lives

We are powerful we have kindness and love
To share to give freely to each other
We have freedom the flight of the dove
Caring for our Mother Father Sister Brother

You are never alone with you I proudly stand
In memory of those who have gone before
I am here my friend my hand within your hand
Their memory imprinted within us forever more

SOCIAL MEDIA BIRTHDAY

Today I become another year older
A day to rememberer in my life's folder
All the messages of happy birthday
Means so much to me in every way

Sometimes I wonder who are these guys
Who I have never met yet seem so wise
Giving advice and just being there
It goes to prove you all really care

So thank you my friends on this social site
For making my day so happy and bright
The wishes and love you all send to me
Makes this an extra special birthday

I will leave you with this I hope you see
That you all mean so much to me
Wishing you all well and happiness
For my friends you deserve no less

HOLIDAY TWINS!

Twins! So cute such a delightful pair
With their mesmerising loveable smiles
Large all seeing eyes their blond wispy hair
I think twins are the best by miles

To have such a lovely wonderful Mum
A Brilliant dad dotes on his daughter and son
An amazing aunty who loves and cares so much
Taking them for walks nappy changes and such

A gorgeous family we were lucky to meet
To see those babies a wondrous treat
As they grow much love they will be given
For their great future you all are driven

Take the time to appreciate your life
Look after yourselves husband and wife
As your family grows all together
Believe in yourselves and love forever

The pleasure has been ours to meet you all
Hopefully we will again when the sea will call
Until that time please accept all our best
Love and life will take care of the rest

LOVE

My love for you overwhelms me so
You make my heart want to sing
Two hearts together each day as we grow
Your love for me the happiness you bring

You bless my life with your heart your soul
My meaning in this world is clear
Your happiness is my one and only goal
To fulfil your dreams forever my dear

On this Valentines day I give to you
My devotion and love my gift forever
My dreams the day we met all came true
For eternity we will love one another

THE TORNADOES OF LOSSIEMOUTH

Farewell the Tornadoes of RAF Lossiemouth
I will miss you though I am from down South
My time I spent at the base years ago
A visit as a young airman in awe of your show

The unforgiving hands of time have passed
In history in memory now you will always last
No longer will we hear the roar in blue skies
The unforgettable sound as you fall and rise

May you be blessed in clouds of pastures new
Be safe in the knowledge I will remember you
So on your new journey you now must go
Fly safe fly true I will see you again from above

AUTUMN

Clear blue skies cold and chilly days
Sunny mornings with cool watery rays
Droplets of frozen dew upon damp grass
Distant memories of the summer now past

Golden leaves adorn the trees
Falling like confetti from above
Darkness comes early on autumn eves
Crackling logs within real fires to love

Autumnal days though they are short
Are the most colourful I always thought
So although winter has almost arrived
This time of year I feel most alive

A LOVE

We have a love that you don't ever see
And i know my darling
You really do love me
why can't they see it too
Why can't they see
How much i love you

Oh my darling
why can't they see
We have a love you don't find everyday
and we share a heart in a special kinda way
our kind of lovin is really rare today
we love each other in a special kinda way

Why can't they see it too
can they see
How much i love you
oh my darling
Why can't they see

Oh why can't they see
Our two hearts together join us as one
We'll be together even when life is done
I love you darling why can't they see

How much i love you and
How much you love me
Why can't they see
Oh why can't they see

WINTER'S END

Freezing winds chill from Eastern shores
Suffocating this land in a blanket of ice
Shivering wildlife cold to their core
An oasis of open water will have to suffice

Harsh snowfalls from a sky dull and grey
Leave their mark smothering the lands
Drifts whipped by the winds in the bay
Unending coldness on faces and hands

Spring will arrive in a week maybe two
When the sun will return once more
Warming lands through and through
Finally green fields will come to the fore

But do not be fooled by the watery heat
For Winter is not far gone from us yet
Not until the sun is high will the freeze retreat
Celebrating early would be something to regret

MARCH

In spring when mother nature comes alive
Daffodils and Tulips gardens begin to thrive
Colourful flower beds are nurtured with care
Blossom on apple trees plum and pear

The cry of a Red Kite can be heard on high
As it soars and lifts upward into the sky
Swooping diving with accurate speed
Searching for carrion on which to feed

Hibernating animals begin to reappear
From their deep sleep at this time of year
Long distance migrators return once more
Flocking on rocks above the rugged shore

LIFE

So sometimes it feels like
life gets us down
Just remember it takes less muscles
to smile than to frown

So when you feel like there is no end
The love within your heart
Any hurt it can mend
Believe in YOU

For you are so strong
You can beat the downs and all the wrong
Never give up and just be you
Life will find a way

Of rewarding you
Take these words I write in your name
Be true to yourself in every way
Life you will find will never be the same
And the love in your heart will stay

GRENFELL

My heart is heavy with sadness and grief
For all the souls of Grenfell Tower
Our eyes watched the horror in disbelief
As a terrible disaster grew by the hour

All the little children the families lost
Sad inconsolable loved ones that survived
This horror comes with unaffordable cost
A community which must be revived

No words will reduce the hurt or pain
I can give you nothing but my pen
Let us hope they passed not in vain
And hope above hope never again

I leave with the hope the sadness you feel
Subsides over the decades of time passing
At the moment it is raw and still so real
So I give to you these words ever lasting

JEANS'S POND

This is the place I learnt to fish
This is the place of my first kiss
This is the place I skipped school
This is the place when life wasn't cruel

This is the place where I had fun
This is the place I met everyone
This is the place where memories were made
This is the place where I was not afraid

This is the place I spent my time
This is the place I wrote this rhyme
This is the place forever in my heart
This is the place right from the start

This is the place I remember my dad
This is the place I am happy and sad
This is the place I now begin to cry
This is the place my childhood began and died

SUNSETS

Clouds on fire with the evening sun
Like molten lava which melts the sky
A jaw dropping sight as the day is done
Gazing upon the awesome sights on high

Amazing colours scattered like embers
lasting memories engraved in our minds
Scenes of beauty for us to remember
Once summer has left us far behind

This awesome earth which we call home
Gifting us with unbelievable sights
Ours to explore discover and roam
Through bright days dark moody nights

Thought provoking sunsets all around
Never fail to make us inspired
The incredible photographs which astound
Of which I will never grow tired

KEV

So my Brother another Birthday arrives
Without you dear Kev in our lives
Among the angels with mum you sleep
Your soul is theirs now forever to keep

I sometimes gaze upon the stars
Wondering if you look upon us from afar
The pain I felt is still deep within me
My heart heavy with your memory

So Happy Birthday Kev I miss you so
Life is different now without you Bro
But I will carry on with courage and love
Which I know you send from above

This day is yours I think of you now
My love I hope you receive somehow
I will not forget you in years to come
Pass my love also to our mum

Time to go Kev but before I do
I need to say this 1 last thing to you
My love for you will never die
We will meet again you mum and I

SPRING

The strength of the springtime sun
has returned to me once more
Replacing the cold of the winter
Warming my soul deep to the core

Blossom explodes into a rainbow of bloom
Grass turns green all across this land
Daffodils return bringing colour to a room
I am taken aback amazed by nature's hand

Days grow longer lighting the night
Early morn brings springs sounds alive
Cold darkness retreats despite its fight
Powder blue clear skies finally arrive

Distant noises resound at the break of dawn
Natures telegraph telling a timeless tale
Waters that were silent come alive with spawn
A deer returns to a well trampled trail

Oh how I have ached for these days to return
Revived by the fresh spring smells in the air
It will not last but to me this is of no concern
As I revel in warm breezes caressing my hair

Welcome back spring you were away too long
Bringing earth's treasures to life once more
Reviving my senses to operatic bird song
Breathing new life to the bare forest floor

MEMORY FADES

I can't remember your face anymore
Or the look in your eyes as before
I didn't even get to say goodbye
You were gone in the blink of an eye

All these years later I am saying goodbye
With a shaking hand and a tear in my eye
For now it is time for me to move on
To live my life this is where I belong

Is there a heaven above I do not know
Nor if there is a hell down below
All I am sure of is that you are not here
Where once you stood close and near

You always said do not live in the past
Never go back it can never last
So here I am moving along
With a renewed strength feeling strong

Goodbye my dear mum you remain in my heart
Because of this we will never be apart
But I must journey forward not back anymore
Though I will never forget you, you can be sure

APRIL

Dark angry clouds carrying life giving rain
Showers fall heavily then clear as quickly again
Blowing in like a fleet of ships upon the sky
Emptying before vanishing in the blink of an eye

Dolphins breach the surface in a secluded bay
Jumping and rolling together they play
With their sleek bodies and powerful tail
Gliding through the water they seamlessly sail

Showers passed giving a break in the weather
Smells of damp earth mix with odour of heather
Misting landscape as the daylight begins to fade
A month like this is how memories are made

I'LL SEE YOU SOON THEN

I'll see you soon then the words were spoken
As you left me with my heart broken
Return to me soon then my dear
Were my last words whispered in your ear

Many years passed following that day
Would we meet again I wish you had stayed
Only time will tell if the truth be known
Every night without you I have felt so alone

Then you returned to me once more
Different somehow the same but raw
The love in your eyes for me had died
I knew you were in there I really tried

But you were lost in deep contemplation
Depressed and sad an awful combination
We rarely spoke of our life before
That fateful day you went to war

The years apart have taken their toll
To find that love again is my only goal
So no matter what has passed before
I know in my heart I love you more

The words you gave me on that last day
Are engraved on my heart and there they stay
We have our own fight and love to mend
For now I whisper I'll see you soon then

OREO

Oreo the pussycat
Was loved by one and all
It would take just a single look
And in love you would surely fall

For Oreo was a beautiful soul
With cuddles and purrs to give
Making everyone happy was his only goal
In the short life he lived

Oreo may be in heaven now
But we still hold him in our heart
We can still hear his soft meow
He may be gone but we will never part

So we remember the lovely Oreo
He really was the best by far
If we want to see him again
we only need to search the stars

ORPHAN

No parents to love or give you care
Alone in the world but do not despair
For there are angels who follow you
Guiding your life on a path that's true

As you grow from a child to a man
You will realise you will do anything you can
To give your love which you never had
And make someone lonely happy not sad

So travel far and spread your wings
Embrace all you see all that life brings
Give your love freely and without walls
Give yourself to all that life calls

Make someone happy like you always will
Remember the sadness of you young life still
No more are you afraid and alone
My child an amazing person you've grown

BULLY

What did I do to deserve what you did
Running scared every day home from school
So frightened I cried as I hid
Beaten to a pulp behind the sports hall

Those days are gone but I think of them still
How I shook when you called my name
That time you caught me on Bluebell Hill
Pushing me to the ground
Was I to blame

I will never forget those terrible days
Being taken and tied to a tree
While you and your mates beat me to a haze
Why did you do what you did to me

RAF

I saw your faces when you beamed with pride
As you watched the parade rifle at my side
That day I was excited no trouble or strife
How did I know it wasn't to be my life

I returned home a sad look on my face
To work and toil I rejoined the rat race
You said you understood but really I knew
How much I had disappointed you

I made my choice which was wrong maybe
All I ever wanted was you again to be proud of me
That didn't happen the way that it should
It never turned out as good as it could

But I promise you this all these years on
Life has led me much time has gone
No change would I make not now not one
Life is not like that what is done is done

ELECTION TIME

So now the election is done
Seats have been lost some have been won
Parliament is again in a complete mess
All juicy stories for the press

But at the end of the day
All will come out in the wash
Some will be glad or so they say
And some will lose a lot of dosh

It doesn't really matter anymore
Some things in the shops will cost more
But it is the truth that matters
Listen up MPs and all you mad hatters

We the people only want what is right
A Great Britain in which we can take pride
For our children to sleep safe at night
And peace across the world far and wide

The End

I hope you have enjoyed my poetry book,
And it has inspired you in some way.
Thank you for taking the time to look,
Maybe there will be a second one day.

For now it is time to let my pen rest,
May your happiness never end.
Wishing all of you the very best,
My love to you all I dearly send.

MJ